Dear Cinny

Thanks for your support and friendship

Mave C

Winning New Customers

As depicted in the cartoon, a new business deal ideally profits both the supplier and the new customer. For an employee, a new customer may mean a raise, a bonus, commissions or a promotion. For an owner, it means profit, hiring new people and increased value in the company. For the customer the new deal means eliminating some of the "pains" and/or a greater profit for the bottom line.

Winning New Customers

by Marc Chabot

MLCIA Publication Inc.

2005

Legal Deposit: National Library of Canada et la Bibliotheque nationale du Québec

Chabot, Marc, 2005 –

Winning New Customers

ISBN 0-97366693-0-6

- Illustrations:	Mario Laliberté
- Web site design:	Radka Losert
- Photo:	André Bouchard of Jostens
- Copy editing:	Anne Fotheringham
- Proofreading:	Anne Fotheringham

Printed and bound in Canada

Published and distributed by:

MLCIA Publication Inc.
50 St-Charles
P.O. Box 26711
Beaconsfield, QC
Canada, H9W 6G7

Dedication

To my unselfish and loving mother, Kathleen,
who dedicated her life to her five children.

Acknowledgments

I wish to thank the people that have encouraged me and helped bring this book to print.

For their generous references:
Ettore Casati Jr., Robert Couteau, Harold Gervais,
Alan Katiya, Jimmy Treybig, Richard Martel,
Shibl Mourad;

For encouragement and help:
Rose Marie Colucci, author and painter;

For help in proofreading:
Cecilia Whiteside and Gaston Beaulieu;

The staff at the Beaconsfield library;

For excellent work in translating the book into French:
Christian Ruby;

For the many hours spent editing:
my friend, David Masse;

For the excellent work producing the marketing plan
for the book, reviewing the book and giving his insights:
my son, Laurier Chabot;

For the many, many hours put towards the structure,
content, graphic design and editing of this book:
my wife, Patricia Wepruk.

Preface

Does the market need another sales book?

I believe it needs a professional sales book that is both practical and practicable. Between these covers, you will find many original ideas and concepts along with some widely accepted sales practices – easily understood, easily applied. All have been time-tested and proven.

Who can benefit from this book?

Everyone can benefit – from professionals (accountants, lawyers, engineers, etc.), executives, managers and salespeople (business development) to recent MBA graduates, all of whom are increasingly being asked to participate in bringing in new business. In today's new economy, employees at all levels are expected to share the responsibility for a company's growth. Recently two CEOs of large firms challenged their executives to call their contacts in order to drum up new business.

Sales managers can use "Winning New Customers" as a training manual, tackling each new element separately and putting it into practice over ten weeks. Salespeople can use it to hone their skills each year just as baseball players do at spring training camp.

The use of humour in the 24 illustrations serves to accentuate the book's main points and its aim is to help readers remember the finer points of selling.

What knowledge can be gained?

Some people are naturals in sales and some people must learn the art of persuasion. If, like most people, you find yourself somewhere in the middle you will need to develop other qualities in order to compete effectively against the superior salesperson.

You will learn about the value of creativity, empathy, finding the customer's pains, dealing with the gatekeeper, the importance of an inside coach, networking, cold calling, etc. Networking and cold calling are of fundamental importance to sales, but few use these "relationship starters" effectively. Other helpful approaches include how to create relationships, work with partners, understand internal politics, and more.

The more things change, the more they remain the same.

Technology has changed the way we approach selling. The Internet, cell phones, personal digital assistants (PDAs), computers and sales software have altered the salesperson's landscape. The Internet provides information about the sales prospect and their competition; it also allows the salesperson to sell from anywhere, anytime. But the basics of "creating a relationship," "selling an idea" and "closing the deal" remain the keys to success.

Acknowledgments
Preface

Table of Contents

Part One   Winning the Customer

Part One

Winning the Customer

Chapter One
The Sales Process

The sales process diagram

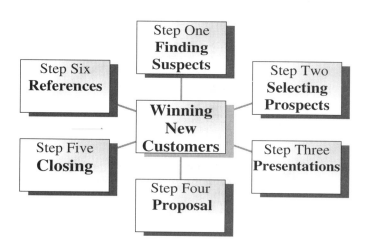

This process is a simple formula of six steps to be followed in sequence and includes qualifying the suspect or prospect between each step.

Until I took my first sales course, I had not viewed selling as a step process and jumped steps or omitted some of them altogether. Understanding and applying the sales process steps helped to boost my sales almost immediately.

Step One – Finding suspects

The sales process begins with finding and selecting a list of suspects who may be in need of your products and/or services.

Qualifying a suspect, the most important first step of your sale, assures you of a suspect's eligibility, desirability and potential as a prospect, and helps to ensure that the process is not a waste of your time and the company's money.

Step Two – Selecting prospects

A qualified prospect is in hand, that is, you have secured a first meeting at which you can present your products and/or service.

At the first meeting, the prospect and the supplier qualify each other. If both agree, another meeting(s) or presentation and/or proposal will take place before long. If you have come prepared with the right questions, both you and your manager will be able to make an informed decision as to the viability of the prospect and whether or not to continue the process.

Step Three – Presentation(s)

A presentation calls for more than merely running through a series of slides featuring your product and/or service. It is a time for gathering information about the prospect's pain(s), finding out which competitors are in the running and taking note of the extent of the prospect's interest in your product or service.

Qualifying continues for both the prospect and salesperson. The inexperienced salesperson may hear a few encouraging words and naively begin to prepare a proposal. More work and another presentation may be needed to sell the prospect on your product or service.

Step Four – Proposal

A proposal is written up when the prospect shows an interest. If accepted, an agreement is signed or a Letter of Intent is given. Most often, at this stage you will discover if you are on the short list or not.

Qualifying continues, if you are in the running, throughout the negotiations. You are told that you are on the short list but you are too expensive or your delivery schedule is too long. Do you have the resources to meet the deadline and will the sale be profitable? What can be done to pull this off? The sales and senior management may be consulted or called in to assist with negotiations.

Step Five – Closing

Final negotiations lead to the signing of an agreement. Everyone has agreed on the terms and delivery dates. The first sale with a prospect is seen as strategic for future sales or spin-offs.

Qualifying after closing entails a review of the process, the implementation procedure and the status of the customer as a reference. Keep informed about production dates and expected delivery, and keep the customer informed at every turn. Promising to deliver goods that cannot meet the customer's deadline or are not ready for the market can quickly become a nightmare, resulting in litigation and loss of reputation. Once lost, a reputation (and the customer) may be lost forever.

Step Six – References

Correct any problems, however minute. Customer satisfaction is essential for repeat business, for building a good reputation in the marketplace and for references. Always ask a satisfied customer to be a reference; references are your best asset when working the next sale.

> *"In the modern world of business, it is useless to be a creative original thinker unless you can also sell what you create. Management cannot be expected to recognize a good idea unless it is presented to them by a good salesman."*
> — **David M. Ogilvy**

Choosing your prospects: Most people can list a dozen or more suspects. We usually gravitate to the one with whom we feel most comfortable or to the most accessible prospect but not necessarily the best. Qualify all and choose to approach those with the most potential first.

Qualifying

One of the biggest fiascos in sales is the lack of qualifying. Qualifying a prospect reduces the likelihood that a salesperson (and management) will spend unnecessarily a month or two and $100,000 or more on a prospect's request for proposal (RFP) or bid only to lose the account in the end. Time spent on the viability of winning the account at any of the first three steps in the process would have been more profitable. In addition, there are the hidden or lost opportunity costs when a sale is not made. This is especially true of any large sale over $500,000.

Do some basic research on the Internet or company Web sites, and carry out a SWOT analysis in order to assess a suspect's Strengths, Weaknesses, Opportunities, and Threats so as not to waste time on risky and ultimately unprofitable deals. Bear in mind that time wasted on a suspect generally means that other opportunities were lost. Before setting up a first meeting with any suspect, it is a good idea to submit the "suspect" company to the scrutiny of sales management and marketing. They are in a position to know if the company:

- Is an old customer, who has been dropped for various reasons;
- Is too small and not in a viable position;
- Has a reputation for not paying; or
- Is another salesperson's account or "belongs" to head office personnel.

At a first meeting and at subsequent meetings or presentations, more information is gathered about the prospect, its industry, customers and competition. With additional research, a more accurate SWOT analysis will help qualify the prospect. The sales process can be stopped at any of the first four steps if it has been determined that:

- A competitor's product has the leading edge in performance and price;
- A competitor is the obvious favourite;
- A prospect is not a desirable customer (too small, too big, unethical, difficult);
- Your company is unable to deliver the goods within the specified time frame; or
- The sale is not considered to be profitable.

On the other hand, be careful about rejecting a prospect that does not appear very promising at first glance.

A true "unpromising" prospect story: A prospect called at a time when only one salesman was in to take the call. Because the salesman had no time to handle the request and the caller had mentioned meeting me, he passed it on to me. This prospect did not look promising at all but I was "hungry." He was unable to meet me and faxed a two-page request for a quote. From this we built a proposal stating the company's needs and our solution to their problems. At that time, the deal was estimated to be somewhere around $500,000 and the company's size was below our radar. However, the contract was eventually signed for over $1 million, and brought in more than $15 million over the next three years.

Rules for qualifying:

1. Deals must be profitable enough to justify the company's investment of time, resources and money.

2. Future potential sales or spin-offs ought to be considered.

3. The prospect must be solid and have a good track record in paying suppliers.

4. Search out the competition, and see if any of them are responding to the RFP.

5. Find out who the incumbent supplier is and why they are not being considered. Is this a bid sent out for the purpose of lowering an incumbent's price?

6. Know the areas in which the competition excels and where your product is superior. Does the competition have a less expensive solution; can you compensate?

7. Does your product address the customer's pains? Do you, or does your competition, have all the solutions to their pains?

8. Your company's resources must be available to do the job within the time frame proposed.

9. Examine the prospect closely for payback and return on investment (ROI) for the customer.

10. Seek out the decision-makers – is it management or users, the CFO or a project leader?

11. Is there a political connection? Are you connected, either inside or outside the company?

12. Find and work with an inside (or outside) coach.

Using your contacts: When we are looking for a job or assistance of any kind, we first ask friends and family. Often we overlook acquaintances and their contacts in our search.

Chapter Two

Making the Contact

When a prospect comes looking for you, the resulting sale is known as a "Blue Bird." This represents less than five per cent of all sales; all others are a product of hard work. Prospects are found through your efforts in networking and cold calling, by way of a telephone inquiry or a satisfied customer singing high praises about your product and service. Your very first step, therefore, is to look to your contacts.

Contacts

Draw on your contacts – family, friends, people at work, school, places of worship, etc. Where do they work? Who do they know? What are their connections? Some of these contacts will be run through quickly when selling a product and may be of little use when selling large, high-cost products or services, such as machinery, computers, software and professional services.

How does one begin to expand the contact base? Join your school's alumni association and the local Chamber of Commerce, attend conferences and seek out events where buyers from the target market can be found. Make a list of associations related to your work. In a list of five to 10 associations, there are plenty of contacts to be made at their conferences, cocktails, annual golf tournaments and other special events, such as benefit concerts. Then again, your primary contacts could be sitting right next to you.

> *A true "contact" story: I overheard our receptionist on the telephone giving out her maiden name. It was somewhat of a rare surname and caught my attention because it was the same as that of a company president I wanted to meet. They were brother and sister. The contact was made and he became a good customer.*

Sometimes simply being a member of an association does not offer enough of a sense of belonging or provide enough opportunities for interaction. I served as a director for seven years of the Canadian Information Processing Society (CIPS), which allowed me to meet some of the most influential people in the industry. CIPS was an important way for me to make contacts and not primarily a means to sell.

Networking

Networking is instrumental in selling within a professional environment. Keep in mind it is not about making sales calls. Sometimes it is making contacts and other times it is building relationships. Networking is not new to most of us, having networked quite naturally in various settings (and for varied reasons) at schools, parties and bars, or wherever a group of people meet.

Half of all sales people network on a minimum level – sparingly even. Another 30 per cent regard themselves as good at networking, but the super salesperson is a wonder to watch as he/she effectively works a crowd. If you need to improve on this skill, read on.

Think of networking as an art to be enjoyed. Search out clubs or volunteer groups of interest or associations related to your industry, and place yourself in the epicentre. Attend as many events as possible so that your face and name become known. To ensure an event will not be a waste of your time, choose the one that gives you the best opportunity to network. Is it a cocktail (room to manoeuvre) or a sit-down meal (time to become acquainted with people)? Who will be attending? If possible, ask for the list of attendees. Check the Web site for the participating partners or organizers and find out if your competition will be there. Come prepared for any scenario.

Networking: **Make contact with potential buyers in the industry by attending cocktails and business luncheons, working with your alumni association or a charity. Networking makes winning new customers so much easier.**

Be as open and friendly as your personality dictates but, above all, be natural. Show genuine interest. Display your best manners. Do include your spouse or partner in the conversation. Do not just talk business (or golf) so as to exclude others. Find common ground for interaction.

Always arrive early for any event. Check the attendees list or the nametags for familiar names. I often chat to the people in charge, remaining at the entrance so as to have an opportunity to meet the arrivals. At times, I have become a self-proclaimed volunteer, directing someone coming off the elevator to the cloakroom as a way of making my first approach. This provides a natural opening for conversation. You may be asked, "Do I know you?" or receive a simple, "Thank you" which may be followed up by exchanging further words in the main room. Mastering small talk is fine, but I prefer asking open-ended questions such as, "What brings you to this event?" and "What are you responsible for in your organization?" Then become a good listener.

If someone is standing apart from everyone else, introduce yourself. Not all important people are comfortable or forward in crowds or artificial settings. And keep in mind that unimportant people can have connections, too. Introduce these people to others, who, in turn, will introduce you to people they know. It may be difficult to focus on more than five people at any one event unless it is an all-day event or extends to a full evening.

If there is a speaker and you have a good question to ask, do so during question period by first introducing yourself and stating your employer's name. In this way, you advertise yourself as well as your company. Even if you do not have a question, it is a good practice to approach the speaker at the end of the speech and introduce yourself for he/she is likely an important person. Leave the speaker with a few words about your thoughts on the talk. On occasion I may offer a document or brochure that I believe could be important to the speaker. My business card is always stapled inside the first page.

When a number of people from your organization are attending the same function, it is preferable to not socialize with each other exclusively. Sit at different tables, if at all possible, in order to maximize your networking potential. If a table is assigned to your organization, verify who is attending and invite someone to fill the empty chairs. In any case, seat yourself at the very last moment so as to continue networking. Between the salad and entrée, take advantage of the break to speak with people at other tables, and at the end, have dessert and coffee with someone else. Warn your tablemates of your intentions and make it clear to them why you have chosen not to be in their company a good part of the evening. They will observe and learn from you.

Stay until the end of the event. There are always stragglers hanging around who may be important. And, once more, I place myself at the table where nametags are now being returned. In this way I am able to meet the people who arrived late or to spot possible prospects that I missed coming in.

> *A true "nametag" story: To clinch a million-dollar deal that I was working on, it was imperative to meet one key player. I offered to help with the guests' returned nametags and met the man. Later that evening he called to say "bring in your team." The deal was signed a few months later.*

The key to meeting an individual is to show an interest, whether in some mutual business venture, helping him in his field or in some personal way. Ask for a business card and follow up the next day with an e-mail acknowledging the meeting. Check the company's Web site to see if you can link them up to someone by introducing them, or be of assistance in any other way. Networking can be played like a hockey game. Pass the puck (help of any kind) and later it may be passed back to you. Less than 50 per cent of the people you help actually return the puck but that's all right. If you network effectively, this percentage of returns may be more than enough.

A true story: If I know someone who is looking for a job, I will look into my contact base to find him a lead or look around an event for a contact. People out of work can be very negative about themselves. Many years ago, I called a friend to tell him about a job opportunity that was perfect for him. After I finished trying to sell him on his ability to do wonders at this job, he thanked me for the encouragement and said that prior to our conversation, he had been thinking of committing suicide. He got the job and did very well.

Outside of scheduled events, networking begins the minute you step out of your front door – at the bus stop, parties, while shopping, at your place of worship, on holidays, talking with new neighbours, or jogging down the street. Keep yourself open to networking in these and all other situations. Once you are comfortable with networking, you are ready to embark on the next chapter and my favourite subject, "cold calling."

"A friendship founded on business is a good deal better than a business founded on friendship."
– **John D. Rockefeller**

Trade shows and conferences

Trade shows and conferences can be the best and worst investment of time and money. It all depends on you and what you make of them. At the beginning of my sales career, I went unprepared and waited for the attendees to walk into my kiosk. Worse still, the business cards were shoved into a corner of my desk and stayed there – unless the opportunity was really solid.

A well-placed kiosk is ideal to catch the eye of anyone entering but occasionally we forgo having one for lack of a suitable location or to save money, and instead decide to work the lanes. Having no kiosk is sometimes preferable to one in an out-of-the-way corner.

Call the organizers or check the Web site to find out which customers, prospects and suppliers will be attending. Arrange plans before the event to have breakfast, lunch or dine with some of them. The big names will have been invited ahead of time in order to attract others and the speakers will have been booked. Often photos of the speakers and the leaders are made available. Memorize these photos and names before the event.

A favourite technique of mine to connect with the leaders, or decision-makers, is to prepare five open-ended questions to ask them, and then, at the end of the survey, present them with a small gift for their time. One of the most successful gifts was a travel alarm clock with my company's logo, which cost five dollars. That was over ten years ago and the one I have still works and is still very practical and stylish.

At a gaming conference, I approached the presidents of lottery organizations from around the world with my survey questions and was followed by the competition's salespeople who were keen to listen in and hear the answers. The questions were basic. What is the lottery's future? What major changes do you see in the industry? What are some of your major pains? Will you be changing your lottery system or introducing new point-of-sale terminals?

Unless you have the best mousetrap, and everyone knows it, there will be periods of time when nothing is happening at the kiosk. Never wait for people to enter your kiosk before speaking to them. Go out and look for people. Meet them in the lanes, visit other kiosks and invite the main players to visit yours or set up an appointment for another time.

Follow up with a standard letter or e-mail message at the earliest date possible while people still have your face and name fresh in their mind. Make an impression by sending an e-mail message that very same evening from your laptop or PDA. Enter all the business cards into a database and follow up your leads with a telephone call within the next few weeks.

Golf and business

Until seven years ago, when I took up playing golf again and joined a golf course, I had been missing out on the most enjoyable part of selling. Golf allows you to exercise in the open air in beautiful surroundings that are conducive to good fellowship, and the networking opportunities are abundant. Most golf courses hold about twenty organized golf-day business events every summer, plus a number of charitable groups sponsor annual golf-day fundraisers.

One successful president told me that he built his company on three games of golf a week. And yet, when I asked thirty university students recently applying for accounting jobs, "Who here plays golf?" no one lifted a hand. Ideally, a marketing course that devotes a few hours to golf etiquette and the importance of golf in business would be beneficial. Being uninformed about the rules of etiquette on the golf course is on par with eating in a high-class restaurant with your fingers.

One Montreal executive, who speaks to many organizations, sees the importance of golf in business and "advises all – men and women – to get their daughters into golf at an early age. Golf will not only help them with their business careers, but will allow them to have a lifelong activity – one that they can enjoy with their spouses well into their golden years, long after their bodies have stopped letting them play demanding sports."

To quote Tanya Maier who has made a business of getting more women, and female executives, to play golf and to use it as a networking tool in Montreal: "As more women enter the pharmaceutical, finance and accounting industries and expand their networks, they need to be part of the game. In a survey done in 2001 by Robert Half International, Executives said that their most successful business meetings were outside the office conducted over a meal. The second most popular place was on the golf course."

Many of my customers and managers were very successful and did not play or care to learn to play, golf. You may feel the same about sports in general. There are obviously other ways to connect in business – luncheons, theatre, shows, etc. But if golf is your sport, and you are not confident about your golf game, take a few lessons, put in some practice time at a driving range and consider making golf a part of your soft sell.

In the last few years, I have been playing almost eighty games of golf every year, some of which are just a short round of nine holes after work that I play for the exercise. For a business golf game, I prefer to arrange a foursome with three senior executives, often CFOs – one is a satisfied customer and the other two are prospects. The satisfied customer almost always gives me a good reference without being aware of it.

Cold calling, Cold: A "cold" cold call is rarely used in professional sales. Usually professional salespeople will know something about the prospect or will have searched the Internet. Nevertheless in exceptional times when there is no other choice, the effort may yet result in a sale.

Chapter Three
Cold Calling

Demystifying cold calling

A cold call is a telephone call or an office visit, during which you present yourself and give your pitch for the purpose of setting up a first meeting. The person you are pitching to does not know you. Many people in sales or business development are uncomfortable with the concept of cold calling and avoid it.

The three categories of professional cold calls are cold, hot and hot-hot. My definition of a "cold" cold call is attempting to speak to a person for the purpose of selling a product or service without a call sheet and little knowledge of the person or company – something akin to those calls we receive at dinner hour from call centres. This is not recommended, but in some situations it is worth a try.

A true "cold" cold call story: A few years ago an appointment at one office brought me to another office across the hall. I asked the receptionist if I might speak to the CFO, having already explained my presence in the building and interest in the company. Since I did not have an appointment, she refused to let me in to see him. Continuing to be polite, I asked for his name and telephone number, left the office and called from across the hall. "Could I have a few minutes of your time, seeing that I am already here... or I can come back at a later time?" The CFO agreed to see me at that time. He liked what he heard and, within two years, we got all his business.

A "hot" cold call is the most common form of cold call. A call sheet has been prepared and some information is known about the person or company before telephoning.

A "hot-hot" cold call is attempted when there is good potential in winning the deal. Preparation is the key. Make use of contacts in the industry and of internal coaches; accumulate information on the suspect's pains, industry, competition and customers. Present a complete solution using your product/service and possibly that of a partner if need be in order to adequately respond to the suspect's concerns. It may take as long as a few weeks before making the call.

Cold calling, Hot: **A "hot" cold call is useful in selling at a professional level. Time and money spent on preparing before telephoning or meeting with a prospect is relative to the size of the potential sale.**

A "hot-hot" cold call that became a cold call:
A potential customer (desperately in need of
my product) had not returned any of my calls
– all of which were "hot-hot" cold calls since I
had thoroughly researched the company,
discovered its information technology (IT)
problems and worked out appealing solutions.
Because the potential customer did not return
my calls, my only option was to make a cold
call. I only had one chance. Without an
appointment, I went into the office well armed,
prepared to bide my time until he was free to
see me. My words to the receptionist showed
my determination, "I am not leaving until I
see Mr. X." Today, these same words could have
you escorted out of the building. Adapt your
phrasing to the times. After an hour, the person
came out and asked what I wanted. I quickly
told him that I knew most of his problems and
had the solutions. Could he give me twenty
minutes? Two hours later I left his office and
the following week, we had a luncheon
appointment for which he paid. He signed the
first order a year later for $10 million.
Eventually the account brought in a total of
$25 million in sales.

In teaching cold calling, I begin by explaining that,
when selling professional services or products, you
are usually talking to another professional. If your
product or service saves the company money or

time, or increases revenues, you are doing this person a favour. In fact, you may make him a hero, help him to get a bonus or be instrumental in his promotion.

For most people a dislike of cold calling stems from the uncertainty of how one will be received. Salespeople are not always regarded as worthy of respect and your skin cannot be too thin. Do your homework first. Research the company's Web site. Determine the company's needs or objectives and how you can meet them. Understand the industry and know something about the person you are calling. Look for people who can give you that information.

> *"It is not rejection itself that people fear, it is the possible consequences of rejection. Preparing to accept those consequences and viewing rejection as a learning experience that will bring you closer to success, will not only help you to conquer the fear of rejection, but help you to appreciate rejection itself."* **– Bo Bennett**

Cold calling, Hot-Hot: A "hot-hot" cold call requires extensive and thorough preparation. The resulting confidence and knowledge of the company and its pains will guarantee a better reception from the prospect during the telephone call or meeting.

Call sheet

Prepare a call sheet with "hot buttons" to get his or her attention within the first 20 seconds. A good opener is to introduce yourself and to give the name of your company followed by "How are you?" Pause for an answer and then quickly introduce the hot buttons:
- "I can save you a million dollars."
- "I can increase your profits."
- "I can reduce your staff and increase your revenue."

Be prepared to back your statements with facts and work out a list of possible responses from the suspect, along with your comebacks. Another hot button is to mention a customer reference within the industry.

Learning to cold call is not difficult, but it requires a bit of work. Spend an hour or two preparing a call sheet and practising until the words feel comfortably your own. Now you are ready to begin. It can take anywhere from an hour to a day to master cold calling. The length of time depends on your level of confidence and how you feel about your product.

Most people in business will be asked to make a cold call sometime in their career, and more and more managers are being expected to bring in new business as well as manage existing business. By keeping in mind that you are doing someone a favour (endeavouring to increase his or her profits), the cold call will then become a "warm" call in no time at all.

Some people that I have trained to cold call turned out to be better at it than me. They had the voice and command of the language and with the necessary confidence they were soon setting up appointments with executives at billion-dollar companies. Recently a tax expert with no sales expertise went through a few hours of training and a month later she had made a few dozen appointments and had closed six new accounts. With preparation and a bit of determination, most people can cold call very successfully.

"An objection is not a rejection; it is simply a request for more information." – **Bo Bennett**

Action list for cold calling:

1. Prepare a list of people and organizations suited to your product and/or services.

2. Research them on their Web sites, the Internet, or any listing of largest companies, public companies, etc. Annual reports and other required disclosure documents are an excellent source of information and are freely available from the U.S. Securities and Exchange Commissions (SEC) Web site (www.sec.gov) and, in Canada, the System for Electronic Document Analysis and Retrieval (SEDAR) Web site (www.sedar.com).

3. Prepare a call sheet script of not more than 30 seconds, with at least two hot buttons included.

4. Practise in front of a mirror and then with another person.

5. Choose a quiet room with no distractions to make your calls.

6. Begin calling when you feel positive. Stop calling if all is not going well. If necessary, go back to Point 4.

7. After getting an appointment, do not stop. Your confidence can be an asset in making the next calls.

8. Have your response ready for comments such as, "I will call you back," "Send me your documentation," "I am happy with my present supplier," "I am too busy at this time."

9. Remember that your objective is to get an appointment.

10. A mentor or friend can help with ideas and encouragement by giving you feedback.

Cold calling at high levels: **An experienced salesperson knows the competition is very likely connected to top management. The chance of success for those who are is very good. To alleviate any apprehension in approaching the higher levels, research the company and its industry and come well prepared to provide solutions to their "pains".**

Calling at high levels

Before making a cold call, become acquainted with the hierarchy of the targeted organization and its leaders. Read the annual report and examine the financial statement. Does the company have an organizational chart of its executives posted on the Web site? Find out who reports to whom. Determine who makes the important decisions – most likely it will be someone at the highest level of the organization.

In the beginning, I lost a few sales when the competition met directly with the chief executive officer (CEO) or financial officer (CFO), president or board of directors. A large computer manufacturer was famous for using this tactic in the hardware industry, and today one of the largest Enterprise Resource Planning (ERP) software companies can attribute its success in part to using this method. Organizations such as large accounting and law firms usually deal only with the board and senior management.

The advantage of working directly with corporate executive officers (CEOs, CFOs, COOs, CIOs, etc.) is that they are in the position of making important decisions and are usually directly involved in the policy-making and decision-making process at the highest levels. Most importantly, they control the money. If they are not directly involved, they usually are aware of the project and can direct you to the right person. If a business deal is initiated with lower-level personnel, it is nearly impossible to step up to any higher echelons without causing a rift in that relationship that could sabotage the sale. Then if any difficulties arise at the implementation stage – as they usually do – lower-level personnel may be less willing to make the project succeed if there are any ill feelings.

In any case, your competition is already "schmoozing" at the higher level. This leaves you dealing with a minion in the organization, pleading your case. The competition has the ear of the top people, making it difficult for them to give the business to an unknown. A solution to this impasse is to have your boss meet with their boss, your CEO meet with their CEO, and so on, depending on the size of the project. Controllers or vice-presidents sometimes have purchasing authority for up to $500,000 worth of goods or services, while commitments of $1 million and more usually require the CFO's approval.

Now that you know where to strike in your targeted organization, the only thing that can hold you back from making sales calls at high levels is fear of the target's high position, fear of saying the wrong thing, fear of messing up with a new prospect. To you, I say, prepare, prepare and prepare! Come well prepared! Know thy customer, his business, his competition, his problems, and the organization and, by all means do a SWOT analysis (Strength, Weaknesses, Opportunities and Threats). If you are providing the prospective client with a solution, saving him money or increasing his profits, you are doing him a favour. With this in mind and armed with the best information, you will find the necessary confidence.

"Drive thy business or it will drive thee."
– **Benjamin Franklin (1706 - 1790)**

Gatekeeper: **An obstacle to reaching the decision-maker is the gatekeeper. The path of the inexperienced salesperson is blocked by the secretary/administrative assistant. One way around the problem is waiting until the gatekeeper has left work; another way is to try to work with him or her.**

Gatekeepers: administrative assistants/ secretaries

Anyone who stands between you and the person you seek is called the "gatekeeper." This is usually the receptionist or the administrative assistant. Being a gatekeeper is part of the job description – to filter calls and take messages – but you can also make them work for you. Even when the barrier appears impenetrable, be polite and understanding.

> *A true story: After telephoning a CFO off and on over a period of six months, I finally got to speak to a live voice instead of the administrative assistant's recorded voice mail. She said it was impossible to meet with the CFO. As she was the nearest person to the top, I made my pitch and asked her if she was a shareholder. I told her that I could save the company millions. She was a shareholder and I knew the company needed cash. She agreed to print out my e-mail for the CFO and he passed the information on to the appropriate people. This gatekeeper helped me with a multi-million-dollar sale without my having to meet with the CFO, and she also helped to save her company millions.*

A way to circumvent the gatekeeper is to call early in the morning, late in the evening or during lunch hour when the target prospect is most likely to be unattended. If you are not able to talk directly to your target prospect, your words will reach him/her through voice mail. Leave a message with your "hot buttons." If the call is not returned, it may mean there is no interest – and then again it may not. Call again, not leaving a message this time, and be persistent until you get to speak to the person you are trying to reach. Keep in mind that everyone is susceptible to bad weeks, year-end closings, vacations and preparing proposals. Allow a few weeks to pass before leaving a second voice mail, indicating that a message had been left earlier but you are not sure if it was received. If your second call does not bear fruit and you still feel strongly that your product or service can save the company a ton of money or increase profits, find someone in your network who can introduce you to the person in question or check the company's Web site for events or shareholder meetings at which the person may be present. Be persistent without appearing like a stalker.

Never forget the importance of the secretary, receptionist and administrative assistant. Treat them with respect and appreciation. They open the door leading to where you want to go. Without coming across "like a salesman," remember them at Christmas, during Secretary's Week, at Valentine's Day, or Easter. Money spent on a choice box of chocolates or flowers can be well spent. This is one of those times when the thought counts more than the gift.

Chapter 4

Getting the Inside Edge

Account planning

An account plan is both the blueprint of an organization and a supplier's master plan for penetrating the organization. To help qualify large prospects and to manage customers there ought to be an account plan in use for each one.

An organizational chart indicates who reports to whom, but on its own, it contains static information. An account plan brings to light relationships and true power. The account plan cites company goals, philosophy and culture. Power struggles, the competitive market and any relevant changes are documented. This information has added value if "war room" meetings are set up from time to time for the purpose of working out objectives, strategies and tactics. After an approach is agreed upon, a potential customer can be asked for his or her input in order to finalize the process.

As reluctant as one may be about spending precious "selling" time in preparing an account plan, the benefits become obvious with time. The salesperson comes to understand the internal workings of the potential customer and the industry, as well as, and sometimes better than, the customer does. An account plan increases the chance of making a sale, and decreases the chance of wasting time by helping the salesperson to focus only on prospects that qualify.

Armed with an account plan for every important prospect and customer, describing the ins and outs of their operations and needs or pains, management has better control of its business. If a sales representative leaves the company, the document is an excellent source of information for a smooth transition with little disruption to the customer-supplier working relationship. Another benefit is the possibility of reviewing an account so as to justify mobilizing costly company resources.

Finding a coach - staying on track

Who is the coach? Almost anyone can be your coach – anyone from an employee to an outside consultant. A coach is someone who has knowledge about the internal workings of the account – what is happening, who the decision-makers are, who is

Finding a coach: A coach inside or outside the organization is an ally who helps you find your way through the company maze. He understands company politics and may know who the real decision-maker is.

for and who is against you – and is willing to pass on information to help you. He/she keeps you up to date on company policy changes, possible structural changes and back-office politics.

This is not cloak-and-dagger stuff. A coach cannot be asked to spy or give you inside information that may compromise him/her or the company. The relationship is an open one and half the time the coach is your main contact inside the company.

It is advantageous to have more than one coach in case you have one, as I did once, who plays both sides. One contact in a large organization represents a one-dimensional point of view, with one opinion and one set of concerns. Two or three contacts on different levels within the company will confirm the political and cultural structure – and help to identify the real decision and policy-maker(s).

A true "coach" story: A president of a company discreetly passed on information to warn me that the new CIO preferred my competitor's computer hardware. He had to stand behind any decision made even though he did not agree. My coach at a lower level had already informed me of the possibility of my computers being thrown out. I had to sell the decision-maker, the new CIO, on the idea that we were the best solution without letting on that I had seen a copy of his biased report and that I knew what he had planned for my computers. I did convince him and my computers stayed. Two months later he was gone.

Recognizing the decision-maker

Working directly with CFOs is a good strategy. Most often, the person who controls the finances is deeply involved in the decision-making process and has the final word. Then again, they may depend on the users or lower management for guidance. Working with organizational charts and knowing who reports to whom is not a guaranteed path to the true decision-maker.

When recognizing that influence and not authority is the force, one must examine interpersonal relationships. Influence is not always visible and can come from the personal friend in the next office as well as from users, independent consultants or different levels of management. Inside coaches are privy to office influencers and can help pinpoint influence in all its forms.

At times, an alleged decision-maker with grandiose ideas will present himself as the one having the final say and block the way to upper management. How disheartening it is to focus on a decision-maker at one level, who is reacting positively to your sales technique, only to come to the realization that the controllers of the company's finances and the final decision-makers are really at another level – one or two steps higher.

Finding the decision-maker: **Without the help of a coach, the identity of the decision-maker is not always obvious. If you have no contacts within the company, attempt to make contact with the CFO first. The CFO sometimes goes under the name of Vice-President of Finance or Controller – the person who controls the money – and can point you in the right direction.**

At this point, the only way to work one's influence to the top and recoup the sale without offending anyone is to involve senior management. An invitation from your top management accepted by their top management to visit your head office and meet your president almost guarantees the sale is yours – at the very least it indicates a strong interest.

Finding the pains

The "pains" of an organization encompass the objectives, obstacles and sore points of its employees. These vary according to the viewpoint of the person within the organization. Ideally one must go on a "pain-finding" mission within the company. At this juncture, it is assumed that the company's industry and competition have been well researched via the Internet, company Web sites and elsewhere.

Develop a set of pertinent questions that require a prospect to think at some length before answering. Accurate information will help the prospect define objectives and goals and lead directly to your strategy and tactics. Every interview should be adapted to the personality of the interviewee – reserved or extroverted, the sceptic or the advocate.

Finding the pains: **Come prepared with open-ended questions. Know the prospect's competition and some of the large customers. Conduct a brainstorming session with an industry expert.**

Questions that engage him or her help build a rapport. Remember the process in your last large purchase and how the salesperson made you feel when your needs were understood. Questions that begin with, "How do you feel about... ," "What do you think about... ," "What is your opinion on...," are ego boosters that make a prospect feel special and comfortable knowing that his or her concerns are of value. They will prolong an interview as well as give you insight.

A question or comment that takes more time to voice than the response is not productive; it shortens the interview. When the attention is on you, it is off the prospect. If relevant, keep it for the end.

It also helps to read between the lines. If conflicting messages are being expressed, confirm what you think you heard by rephrasing it in your own words to ensure your understanding. A good grasp of another's ideas promotes trust and establishes a good relationship. Confirm what you hear by summarizing the main points at a transition point in the questioning or at the end of the interview in as few words as possible.

Listen more and speak less. Concentrate on the words, the tone and underlying messages. Be still; avoid unnecessary movements that can be distracting. And always be pleasant and enthusiastic.

Whatever you are selling, your product or service may not be sufficient to deal with every customer's pains. It may be inconvenient to bring a partner on board, but the key is to win the business, especially if the competition's solution is complete (with or without a partner). See Chapter Eight on partnerships.

"Successful people ask better questions, and as a result, they get better answers."

– Anthony Robbins

Chapter Five
Getting the Outside Edge

What is the competition doing?

Know thy enemy. Study his product and his strategy in winning accounts. Once you understand your competition, you have an advantage. Then do your own strategizing. One of the pleasures in selling can be outsmarting the competition.

Be aware of the competitor's position in the account in relation to you. One way to take the lead is to alter the usual way of doing things; for example, offer an unsolicited proposal and influence the request for quote by featuring what your product has and your competition does not.

What is the competition doing? **Most large companies do competitive analysis. To do your own, check the Web often for information on who competes in what field. Ask a customer or prospect about your competition, find out who is wooing them and talk to the competition at any event where you may meet them.**

Your presentations can play up your product's strengths and your competitor's weaknesses – with subtlety and without naming names. Direct criticism can have adverse effects, especially if directed against an established supplier. Place the competitor in a reactionary position, explaining and justifying his product or service while you remain the professional. Always appear to take the high road and never knock the competition.

> *A true "lost sale" story: A customer asked for the contract by Friday afternoon but he agreed to accept it Monday morning. The competition presented theirs that Friday, invited the customer to play golf and sealed the deal on the 19th hole.*

Be first in the game to get control of the account. Be early and be there before the competition, whether it is meeting higher management or giving the first presentation.

> *"Observe your enemies, for they first find out your faults."* – **Antisthenes (445 BC - 365 BC)**

How do outsiders view the prospect?

Not all prospects are desirable customers. Some can drain resources, reflect badly on their supplier and have reputations for improper procedures or poor paying habits. A company's financial statement and/ or annual report provides only a partial, and usually a subjective, view of a company.

If possible, speak to a prospect's customers and suppliers. Keep abreast of anything going on in the industry that concerns your prospect, by reading the daily newspapers and business magazines. Immerse yourself in the business, joining a related association if there is one, so as to be able to speak intelligently to senior management about their concerns.

To complete a profile of the company, attend shareholder meetings where objectives and objections are voiced. An added bonus is that shareholder meetings provide an excellent opportunity to network, allowing you to hobnob with the CEO and CFO. More often than not, a number of people on the board of directors are CEOs of other companies.

Chapter Six
Presentations,
Proposals and Closing

Presentations

We have all sat through good and bad presentations – and many fell someplace in between. The main criteria for a good presentation are to keep people awake and listening and to convey a message in a minimum of words. Stick to the valid points. Less is more – and better.

The best presentations from the viewpoint of a customer are those that focus on the customer's problems and objectives and show how your product and/or service provide the answers. Search out the prospective customer's Web site and research the company, its competition and the industry. Do a check on your preferred search engine before asking anybody questions.

It goes without saying that the presenter can add value to the presentation by being an effective speaker who engages the audience. PowerPoint has simplified the process of making slides but has done little to improve presenters. Some presenters rely totally on their slides and read their way through their allotted time. Slides are to be used as a reference to help carry the speaker from one point to another in a coherent pattern with a beginning, middle and an end, and with a sense of progression. Limit the slides to 20 if practical, advancing approximately every minute from one to the next.

Use pictures, humour and customer reference stories. Include one or two personal stories. If you have practised well, you will feel more confident and this will influence the effectiveness of the presentation.

Prepare well and be ready for any eventuality. Practise and finalize your presentation a day or two before. Arrive early, allowing one hour for a set-up. Your gear should be checked at home or the office and you should do a final practice run-through that day. Carry extra diskettes, CD-ROMs or USB drives, one in your luggage, the other on your person. Lost luggage or a stolen laptop should not be the reason for losing a sale.

A true "presentation" story: A friend was to present in another city and left his power supply cable at home. On the plane he used up his batteries. On site there was no similar power supply to be found. You do not want to know the rest of the story.

Besides setting time aside at the end for the question period, always allow enough time to let your customer speak. Find out if you missed something or something new is on his/her mind. Determine how effectively the people in the room view your solution. Is anyone animated... or smiling? How many people have come forward to speak to you? How many questions have been asked? Are you alone at the end of the presentation? This is another opportunity to qualify a prospect.

If being well prepared does not inspire you with enough confidence to stand and talk in front of a group of people, consider enrolling in an introductory Dale Carnegie course and the Toastmasters program.

A true "shy-to-confident" story: As a systems analyst in my mid-twenties I gave my first presentation red-faced and stuttering. My understanding boss recommended the Dale Carnegie course. In eight weeks I changed from somewhat of an introvert to an extrovert.

The introductory Dale Carnegie course is the most attended program in the world. If shyness and confidence are not your problem but you still have an overwhelming fear of giving a presentation or speech, there is Toastmasters. This organization has more than 8,000 clubs around the world, and the larger cities have more than one chapter, making it easy to find a group.

The cost to join is approximately $100 per year. You may attend as a guest as often as you wish before joining. Within a year, you will have made a few friends and learned many more skills than just public speaking. You will have learned to conduct meetings and give impromptu speeches, one of the more popular activities, all done in an encouraging, non-critical forum. Toastmasters also offers advanced courses on motivational speaking and management.

"Effective communication is 20% what you know and 80% how you feel about what you know."
— **Jim Rohn**

The proposal

The proposal must resolve the customer's needs, problems and pains. The simplest and most effective method is one that follows the request for proposal (RFP) guidelines, and mirrors the customer's objectives with your solutions. In a good economy, the end user has the power to spend; in a recession, the CFO often decides – payback and return on investment (ROI) need to be addressed.

A good deal of work must go into the executive summary with a focus on how the prospect's concerns are being addressed within their budget. Of secondary importance is the type of proposal you and your organization choose to use – short and succinct, or detailed and covering over a hundred pages, printed on glossy paper or regular. The customer's primary concern and immediate focus will be the content of the executive summary and the cost of the product and/or services.

The style of proposal ought to reflect the effort that was made in putting it together. "Boilerplate" proposals are as unimpressive as those containing three inches of paper filled with "cut and paste" paragraphs taken from old proposals. A professional-looking document that contains a winning strategy focusing on the customer's objectives will be a winning proposal.

A true "winning proposal" story: After winning a multi-million-dollar account, we learned that our closest competitor's bid was 40 per cent below ours and that the customer had asked the other contenders to re-submit their proposals to answer the needs. The competition had obviously failed to understand this and had submitted boilerplate proposals – and lost the bid.

An ideal proposal is one that is "wired," that is to say it is phrased in a way that it favours one product or service. If an RFP unexpectedly lands on your desk, it may well be that a competitor has already sold the prospect on his solution and the prospective customer is either using the RFP as a bargaining tool, or is required by company policy regulations to send out for other bids. Organizations sometimes wish to show an open policy by appearing to go after the best deal, but will ultimately go with their favourite supplier and disregard all others – unless something unforeseen occurs.

A true "losing proposal" story: A salesperson spent three months and over $100,000 on an RFP that arrived from out of the blue, but appeared to be wired for our company. We lost. It turned out that the firm had no intentions of switching technologies, but was obligated to call for bids. Later we discovered that our proposal cost the "winning" supplier millions. Our competitor feared losing a third account to us in six months, and felt obliged to lower the bid to ensure winning the sale.

The three possible outcomes at the end of the proposal stage are signing an agreement (or receiving a Letter of Intent), discovering you are on the short list or learning you have lost the bid. If you are still in the running, qualifying this prospect continues. Is the bid profitable, can you deliver the goods on time and is the prospect still a desirable customer?

Unsolicited proposals

Imagine the position of a customer who receives a document from a supplier describing the company's concerns and appearing to understand its future objectives. It offers solutions that are compatible with the workings of the company and its strategy. Would he/she be impressed? Impressed enough to deal with the supplier.

But beware of the temptation of committing to a complex proposal on the basis of a few encouraging words. A two-page proposal is insignificant but large sales require proportionately larger proposals, which almost always consume a lot of resources, time and money. Is it worth it? If, after studying the prospective customer and the industry, you have the necessary confidence that your product answers the prospect's concerns, ask senior management for their approval. Their experience will help decide whether a proposal is capable of winning the customer or not.

In some circumstances the cost of an unsolicited proposal can be spread over a number of prospects in the same industry – tailoring it to the specific company with a few minor amendments. In all cases, the person who receives the proposal must be in a position of some authority – a CEO in some cases.

Closing and negotiating

You are now near to closing a deal. In some large sales, the customer has a major input in the step-by-step sales process and consensus is reached during negotiations. In this type of sale, your role is that of a consultant – your proposals are weighed and decided upon by the customer.

If the relationship with your prospective customer is a close one, the negotiating stage is that of two friends working together in complete trust. As simple and utopian as it sounds, a lot of time, hard work and mutually rewarding experiences have gone into the relationship long before reaching this stage.

Now let's get back to reality. It's negotiating time. There are companies out there that pride themselves on their negotiating skills. To them, all is fair in love and war and business. Take a course on negotiations early in your sales career. It can also serve you well in your personal life when buying a house or a car.

Negotiations: **If you are not an experienced negotiator, take a course, read books on negotiating and/or seek advice from a senior person in your organization. Otherwise you may pay a hefty price when closing deals.**

Closing the deal: **Some salespeople focus on getting the contract not really knowing if it is possible to do the job on time or if it is profitable. This is usually considered the most complex part of the sales process. If each step in the sales process has been followed the customer and you, as a consultant, have made the decision together.**

A true "negotiating" story: One such customer waited until year-end (when my company was trying to meet its sales forecast) and out-negotiated my two levels of bosses. Later, at lunch, a contact within the company revealed that they had all just completed a one-day course on negotiation and offered me information on it. In subsequent dealings, I learned from them and often came out the winner. At times they discussed their methods of winning in front of me and they almost felt sorry for some of their suppliers. I certainly did.

Customer references

The sales process is nearing its end. The product has been delivered on time, installed and tested. Any problems, major and minor have been corrected. Now is the time to ask the customer to be a reference.

The easiest path to making a sale is via a good customer reference and it need not be your own customer – one from another salesperson will do. An increasing number of companies, especially those in the software business, stipulate in their contracts that the customer agrees to act as a reference and to accept site visits. The astute new customer can regard this stipulation as a guarantee of good service to come. Existing customers can also be approached for references and for permission to have visitors on site at their convenience.

Customer references: **A satisfied customer, who has been well treated, returns the favour by telling others about your great product and/or service.**

A technique that I learned from observing successful salespeople was to make a first sale in a specialized industry, obtain a good reference from this sale and go on to sell to others in that same industry, using the first customer as a reference. A happy customer is your personal spokesperson and your best advertisement.

A true "customer reference" story: Early in my career, one good customer questioned why he was not being used as a reference. Eventually a prospective customer was brought to his premises but he refused to allow the prospect into the computer room. When I called him later, I learned that the computer had been down and since this customer knew that I was trying to sell the prospect a non-stop computer, he saved me from having to explain why the fail-safe system had failed. This customer's reference and business acumen was key to winning over the prospect, and led to the eventual sale.

By this time the above customer and I were in a truly symbiotic relationship, in which I sometimes stepped into the role of consultant and headhunter, and in return, the customer bought my PCs rather than some lower-priced ones on the market.

"In sales, a referral is the key to the door of resistance." – **Bo Bennett**

Part Two

Customer Care
and
Partners

Chapter Seven
Taking Care of the Customer

The importance of happy customers

It has been said, "It is seven times more expensive to convert a new prospect into a customer than to retain a good customer." The assets or jewels of any company are its customers, owing to their importance as good references and their repeat business. A few companies rely solely on customer satisfaction. These companies have no need for a sales force because their sales are made by word of mouth (references) or repeat business.

If it is true that 80 per cent of new business comes from the 20 per cent of existing customers, it is wise to regard the established customer as one would a cherished friend. Set up regular meetings on a formal basis and drop by from time to time to re-acquaint yourself with the staff and management on an informal basis.

Taking care of the customer: **Spending time with a customer inside and outside the workplace is essential to building a good relationship. From these occasions come repeat orders and good references. So spoil the customer.**

Keeping your good customers happy

A true "working for the customer" story: A technician brought to my attention a customer's high telecommunication costs. I did a little research and then went to the president and said, "Every month you withdraw $40,000 in cash from the bank and then you go out and drop it down the sewer." That analogy certainly got his attention. The company made some of the suggested changes and eventually saved $80,000 a month.

When you show interest in helping your customer's business grow by understanding their industry, finding alternative solutions and passing up on extra commissions when the alternative is best for the customer, you have a customer for life.

A true "unhappy customer" story: In order to make quarter-end figures, a company had computers shipped to the customer's warehouse where they sat until needed. I joined the company six months later and was given this customer as part of my base. At that point, not one of those computers worked and no one in the office wanted to take care of the customer because the commissions had already been paid to the departing salesman. It took four months to turn the account around. The fallout from this disaster may never be known, but the time, effort and resources spent on rectifying that one mistake proved costly.

Listening to the customer's needs: **Often we do not listen carefully enough or know how to listen, or worse, ignore customers when they talk about their pains.**

Before reaching these depths with a customer, use the following pointers to keep your customers happy and to prevent them from looking elsewhere.

1. Prepare an account plan for each customer if one does not already exist. (See Account Planning.) An account plan of two pages is sufficient for small customers while large national accounts may require up to a hundred pages.

2. Keep abreast of any problems, issues or change of staff. A new project leader or manager, who is more likely to be familiar with a competitor's product, may need to be sold on your product. Plan meetings with decision-makers, such as the CEO or CFO, in order to get the pulse of the company.

3. Introduce your customers to others in your network who might give them new business or become a partner.

4. Consider putting together a team and preparing a SWOT analysis (Strengths, Weaknesses, Opportunities and Threats).

5. Work on forming a good relationship with the decision-makers outside of business hours; i.e., take in a football or hockey game, boxing match or any other sporting event, invite them to a dinner or an evening with respective spouses, arrange a foursome

for a golf game, etc. In a relaxed informal setting, less important company matters or personal concerns may be mentioned. You learn to understand each other's personalities better, making it easier to "read the signs" during serious meetings. You may also hear how the competition is doing or messing up.

6. Look for opportunities to help your customers. Can your company buy their products or services? Nothing is more out of sync than winning a big account and being yourself a customer of one of their competitors. Be a headhunter when needed. Introduce your customer to good people suitable for any open position, from clerical staff to management. Both the employee and the customer will be appreciative and tend to be more accommodating in a crisis. Look out for ways to save them money, and not just with upgrades and products that add to your commissions. Take on the company's concerns. If they do well, so do you with more sales, more commissions and stronger references.

"I always use my clients' products. This is not toady-ism, but elementary good manners."
                                   – David Ogilvy

Chapter Eight

Partnerships

Importance of partners

Forming partnerships or alliances is another type of sales strategy. These relationships can offer valuable insight into a sales prospect and tend to open up markets otherwise inaccessible to either partner acting alone. Good partners maintain their autonomy but work together to achieve a variety of goals beneficial to both – a truly symbiotic relationship, each looking out for their partner as well as for themselves. Some companies rely on partnerships rather than a sales force to sell their product.

Many companies that specialize in a given field find that their means and ability to sell their products and services are limited by geographic scope as well as by the number of possible clients. To increase sales, the company will seek partners in order to expand their field of prospects. The field may be widened with a partner who has a compatible product, enhances the service, improves delivery or increases exposure to the marketplace by association.

Large-scale projects demand extra financing and manpower that only large firms can provide. Packaging your product with another's services allows you to compete in a wider range of projects.For example, I found it easier to sell large computers when they were bundled with a software solution.

"The political tradition of ancient thought, filtered in Italy by Machiavelli, says one thing clearly: every prince needs allies, and the bigger the responsibility, the more allies he needs."

– **Silvio Berlusconi**

Partners working together: **To offer a complete solution to a prospect or customer's requirements, to access new markets or simply to increase earnings, a partnership can be a valuable sales strategy. Finding partners is much like building friendships, and both can be mutually beneficial.**

Types of partners and where to find them

Smaller companies that cannot afford salespeople in other countries have agents or resellers to represent them. Accounting firms and law firms, headhunters and management consultants have working agreements with similar firms in neighbouring cities or other parts of the world. A good customer reference is also, in essence, a good partner.

In my role as a partnership manager for a hardware company, I approached software companies to enter into partnership relationships, and searched out other companies to act as agents, original equipment manufacturers (OEMs), or resellers. My role was still that of a salesperson – to make the partners happy and profitable, as I would any customer.

With a bit of imagination, partners can be found in a variety of places. Trade shows are one of the richest places to find new partners and to help existing partners find new customers. (See Chapter Two on trade shows and conferences.) Another fertile hunting ground is your university alumni associations. Alumni events are a good place to meet another set of people outside your usual contacts in the business world. Graduates making their mark in an industry are often invited to speak about their successes at alumni association events. Participation in the alumni association offers an excellent

Honesty: **Honesty has always been the best policy. Good principles are the foundation for continued sales success, and exaggeration is to be avoided. Tell it like it is.**

opportunity to meet these highly successful and influential people and gain the best entry point to the companies they have built. Universities also make great partners, often working with companies in research and development projects.

> *A true "resourceful" story: A CEO was looking to increase sales and asked the executives to do some searching among their contacts for new customers. One executive approached a good supplier and asked to meet their CEO to get the business.*

A good customer can become a partner if its customer base has value as an important prospect base for you. In turn, look up your suppliers and assess which ones have the makings of a partner or customer. If possible, buy a partner's product or service. Even at a higher cost, purchasing the partner's product should be seriously considered in order to establish and maintain a good relationship.

> *A true "give and take" story: The sales process had reached its closing stage but the COO would not sign the million-dollar contract until he received an acknowledgement that we would buy their products. As unhappy as my COO was about the demand at the time, the relationship turned out to be a very fruitful one. A few years later they won our award for best supplier.*

As with any legal document, a partnership agreement requires that great care be taken when writing it to ensure elimination of any possible misunderstandings over issues such as payments,company direction, overlaps in bidding for the same sale and general expectations. An important clause to include is a specified time frame for the partnership. An unproductive partner can be a weight or an obstacle to other relationships. A more important section is to have a committed budget and resources set aside for the partnership. Regular communication between key people from both partners will help to maintain a good partnership for as long as it continues to benefit both organizations.

"If we are together nothing is impossible. If we are divided all will fail." – **Winston Churchill**

Part Three

The Salesperson and Selling

Chapter Nine

The Professional
<u>Salesperson</u>

What it takes to be a professional salesperson

A sales professional typically may have graduated from university with a degree in arts or sciences, engineering, law, commerce, or any other discipline or course of study you can imagine. Then again, many do not have a university background, but have acquired important technical skills or expertise in a specific profession. The true common denominator is that he or she sells to other professionals, and occasionally directly to consumers (for example, big ticket items such as private aircraft for CEOs or royalty). Professional sales may vary from $50,000 to $100 million or more.

Most professional salespeople have worked their way up to larger sales only after building up experience and confidence by selling products or services on a smaller scale, and expanding their network in a particular field. For example, an inexperienced real estate agent will begin selling smaller houses, gradually moving up to larger homes, eventually handling higher-end waterfront properties and then perhaps will jump into selling commercial properties. Occasionally you meet a person with a privileged network who has jumped the queue and gone directly into selling private jets.

My observation of the general sales force has been that, out of ten salespeople, two did not belong in sales, two were outstanding and the rest were average. Some of the average salespeople definitely had the potential to rise, while others were more or less limited as they lacked certain key facets of selling that cannot be learned, such as genuinely liking people, having the capacity to endure long sales cycles and a passion for sales.

It is easier to sell to someone with an agreeable personality, but not everyone has the time or the patience to look for the good that can always be found in the most contrary persons. Many of my customers became good friends as well as good references. If at all possible, stay away from prospects that are difficult to like. The feeling would probably be mutual and the result is likely to be unproductive.

You have to be able to endure the long process of working towards a large sale with no assurances of winning. Endurance and assurance comes with confidence built up over time, both as a result of successful sales and the experience gained from unsuccessful sales. One of my long-time friends, Sylvain Tetreault, is the most persistent salesperson I have known. In one case, even after a competitor won the sale, he maintained a good relationship with the customer and finally won a $10-million contract when his competitor eventually messed up.

Credibility and selling go hand in hand. It is a tenuous connection. A relationship based on trust brings with it over time a sense of customer loyalty. Stretch the truth; tell a little white lie once and a person's perception of you can quickly change and affect future business deals. Without trust a salesperson cannot sell a product. The standard in sales ethics can be a variable; therefore the strongest ethical value sense needs to guide your actions. If you make a mistake, own up to it immediately.

An advertisement for sales personnel ought to ask, "Do you have a passion for sales?" Enthusiasm can sometimes make up for shortcomings in sales technique. Enthusiasm is also infectious. Without it, you can hardly interest a prospect in your product. In order to sound genuine one has to choose the company and product that will light that fire. It will be reflected in the tone of your voice and your body language.

You have the making of a good salesperson if you have the following qualities and abilities:

- Facility to like the people to whom you sell
- Endurance and perseverance
- Confidence and assurance
- Trustworthiness and high sales ethics
- Good amount of passion for sales

Like actors or athletes, the more successful you are, the more money you make. The difference in sales is that you are a hero on the last day of the year for making your numbers, but on the following day (the first day of the new fiscal year), you are just another salesperson with a bigger quota. There are tough hurdles to jump every day, and there are disappointing days when a demo fails to work or a big sale that has been in the works for a year is lost.

A career in sales is one of the most rewarding careers. No other job gives you the flexibility, the creativity, and the money for so little effort.

"Nothing great in the world has been accomplished without passion." **Georg Wilhelm (O Magazine, September 2003)**

Why become a salesperson? A job in sales offers advancement, flexible hours, creativity, good earnings, challenges and more. It calls for endurance, perseverance and confidence. It is never static.

Why be a professional salesperson?

Sales – is it a sought-after profession on the same footing as engineering, medicine or law? Few people grow up aspiring to be in sales. Often, our experience as customers with salespeople is that they sell a bill of goods without any regard for our needs, satisfaction, or future relationships. So what can change your mind?

> *A true story: A professor of marketing and sales at Concordia University was lecturing one evening on professional sales and how salespeople were necessary for companies to prosper and for the economy to grow. He told a story about introducing himself to a fellow passenger in business class, who happened to be the president of a company, and proud of it. When he said he was a salesman, he got the cold shoulder. Upon leaving the plane, our professor asked the president how much he earned and he replied with pride that his salary was $25,000. (Bear in mind that this was in the early 1970s.) Our professor informed him that he earned $50,000 a year and then, with an air of confidence, went on his way.*

Money. A good professional salesperson can earn a very good income. At one sales rally, our president introduced us to a tiny young woman and said she had made more money than he did that year – more than $500,000. Victoria only got her start after having begged three different sales managers for a job in sales. One of them finally agreed to give her a chance. In the software industry (especially in enterprise resource planning [ERP] software), in commercial real estate, insurance, finance (stock brokerages), etc., it is not uncommon for the top salesperson to earn a $1 million a year. You may be top sales material and not even know it.

Flexibility. Despite the constraints of having to bring in a substantial yearly quota, your schedule is often arranged for your convenience. You work when and how you wish to work. As a golfer, setting up foursomes with good customers and serious prospects may be more beneficial than sitting in the office making telephone calls. If the sun is shining some afternoon, you have the option of spending time with your favourite customer, prospect or friend on the golf course. If golf isn't your thing and if there is enough wind, you can invite someone along for a fine afternoon of sailing. Managers and the rest of the staff do not always have these options.

Creativity. Selling is an art. Most of my large deals were won with some creative strategy. Something extra is required in creating a winning proposal that goes beyond merely solving the problems a customer has put forward. Sometimes an idea comes from checking the prospect's Web site, researching the competition, or finding an internal coach who will give you the inside scoop on the prospect's needs. Other times, it takes being a bit of a maverick and not accepting the way things have always been done.

Challenge. Closing a large deal is akin to running a marathon in that it takes long preparation and hard work that pays off with a similar high.

Recognition. Along with the money comes membership in the million-dollar club that recognizes the contributions of top salespeople. You and your spouse (or significant other), along with the best of the sales force are sent to a paradise in the south or to a European destination where you are treated to elaborate dinners, celebrity guest speakers, entertainment and surprise packages left on the pillow every night. The very best of the best salespeople are chosen to sit on the president's council where they meet with the president to discuss strategy a few times a year.

Advancement. Many presidents and other senior executives with high tech or other companies have had a stint in sales. A successful career in sales is often rewarded with a position in senior management. To promote your own business, you also need to have practised selling.

"Only passions, great passions, can elevate the soul to great things." – **Denis Diderot (1713-1784)**

Time management: **Time is a fleeting commodity. It is far easier to allow events to decide your next actions but more practical and rewarding to plan them.**

Chapter Ten

Developing Sales Skills

Time management

Twelve years ago I took a time management course and discovered that 30 per cent of my day was unproductive. Procrastination was the main culprit, encouraged by the ringing telephone, e-mails and invitations from fellow employees in the neighbouring cubicles to go for coffee.

The office setting can promote wasting time. It is best used only for sales meetings and preparing proposals. Avoid large office meetings if possible. It is preferable to meet one-on-one for a more productive outcome. Answer e-mails and prepare expense reports outside of office hours. I was told that one of the most successful salespeople at IBM in Montreal was never seen at his desk during office hours.

Do not give in to procrastination – take action and "just do it" instead of thinking about it for hours or days on end. This attitude works a good part of the time and gives one a wonderful feeling of satisfaction. A whiteboard installed in a central spot in your home is useful for jotting down "things to do," reminders or ideas that spring to mind without warning at any hour of the day or night. The "writing on the wall" demands attention simply by being seen repeatedly.

A good use of time is setting aside fifteen minutes to arrive early for an appointment. This avoids any extra stress and allows time to organize one's thoughts. Check around the reception area – if there is a sign-in book, look to see if a competitor has made a visit recently. One can often learn a good deal from talking to the receptionist. A telephone call made hours or a day before to confirm the meeting ensures that the trip will not be a waste of time.

Use gadgets available in the marketplace to help you work more efficiently. If your typing is limited to two fingers, try voice recognition software. Organize your day with a personal digital assistant (PDA) using the calendar and the to-do list, and categorize the items in terms of importance. Prioritizing your tasks helps you to keep on track.

A cell phone with a good hands-free device helps increase my productivity. During a forty-five minute commute to and from work while sitting in traffic, I make and return calls, confirm that day's appointments, and set up new appointments.

> *"It has been my observation that most people get ahead during the time that others waste time"*
> – **Henry Ford**

Empathy and body language

I first looked up the word empathy when my employer told me I had scored high on empathy on their sales test. One definition of empathy is the capacity for participating in the feelings and ideas of others. In other words, it is putting yourself in other people's shoes, or listening to and understanding what a customer is saying and feeling. This goes far beyond just hearing words.

In sales, empathy encompasses the concerns of the customer. A salesperson with empathy understands the customer, what the customer is trying to explain and what he is feeling. His primary motivation is the welfare of the company. At times, a salesperson may side with the customer rather than with his own company – but never to the detriment of his company or job. When a customer and the employees relate to a salesperson as if he were another employee, it is due to the empathy displayed by that salesperson.

Empathy can be developed with, or be enhanced by, an ability to read body language. As in music, some people have "perfect pitch" and can play without looking at sheet music while others must learn the notes and practise. Find a book in the library on body language and have some fun experimenting by interpreting up to 30 different movements or actions – positive and negative. Look

Empathy: **Not everyone is capable of putting themselves in someone else's shoes. It can be painful as well as difficult.**

upon it as a game and test your ability to read the darting eyes (lies), hand motions (nervous or confident), placement of arms and legs (open or reserved). Remember, however, crossed arms may be nothing more than a comfortable position.

Body language is unspoken communication that can reveal something about a person's true feelings, and may be conveying the direct opposite position than that expressed by their spoken words. No matter where you are on the empathy spectrum, with practice you can increase your awareness of the undercurrents in a room or can decipher what someone is really saying and act on it accordingly. Most messages are communicated this way and correctly reading body language can alter the outcome of a meeting. If a prospect does not warm up to you, it is unlikely that he or she will buy from you, and there is a good chance that you may be wasting your time. A good indicator of how you are perceived is the smile. Is there a response to your smile? Are their teeth showing?

At the same time, be aware that while you are interpreting a customer's nonverbal signs, yours may be screaming out messages that are best hidden. The tendency to smile back when someone smiles at you is also true about other emotions or reactions. If you come across as guarded and reserved, it is unlikely that a prospect will warm up and open up to you.

Body language: **A prospect's body language may be more revealing than her words. She scratched the top of her head and looked away but she did not cite any problems. There may be different interpretations of these actions.**

Recycling

Recycle yourself to improve skills or gain new ones so that you stay on top of your game. Stagnation is sitting on one's laurels and that is the slippery slope to obsolescence. Take courses offered by your company or special courses suited for advancement in your job. Companies look favourably on employees who endeavour to improve themselves, even if it involves a skill indirectly connected to work.

Salespeople would do well to recycle themselves each year and when times dictate, just as baseball players do at spring training camp.

A true "personal recycling" story: I changed jobs from one in which I had carved out a comfortable niche and had everything done for me (though I did get my own coffee and sometimes even made the coffee), to another where I was expected to do my own typing, send e-mails, make copies and write proposals. The world had changed and reality struck hard. I took summer classes at a local school and learned to make spreadsheets, prepare presentation material, learned about the Internet, etc. I vowed never to fall behind again, but to stay ahead of the curve.

Visit the library or bookstore often to look for books on sales and marketing; applying only two or three pointers from each source will increase your productivity. The outcome of regularly recycling yourself is often winning new customers. With more skills, widening interests, recycling can also keep you employable in a variety of career choices.

> *"I know of no more encouraging fact than the unquestioned ability of a man to elevate his life by conscious endeavour."*
> – Henry David Thoreau (1817–1862)

Failure in sales

No one likes to talk about his or her failures but from failure we learn. I had more than my fair share and hung on long enough to have learned a lot.

My very first mistake after deciding on a sales career was to work for the wrong companies. After experiencing bad management, dishonesty and obsolete sales products, I saw the importance of checking out the company's culture, their management and researching their products and services in the marketplace.

Tandem Computers was a good company for me. Its relatively new and unique product was a tough sell in a niche market and the competition was IBM and Hewlett Packard – established companies with solid reputations and well-trained people. But their product lit the fire in me.

I continued to learn from my mistakes. My boss told me not to return to my old sales "pasture"; there would be no sales there. I paid calls to old customers where I had experienced success before and where I was most comfortable. I was told to focus and instead I gave 36 presentations in three months. My boss demanded that I choose only six prospects and work on closing them. With my job in this fantastic company in jeopardy, I had little choice but to focus. Within two quarters, I closed five accounts.

Prepare to fail and learn for up to two years before mastering the necessary skills. Observe from the successful salespeople around you and ask them to mentor you. As Tandem was a new company and I was the first salesperson hired in Montreal, there was no one to make those mistakes from which I could learn, except me.

Half of the salespeople hired left within a year rather than stay and learn. Their biggest failure was not qualifying a prospect, calling too low in a company's hierarchy and not taking the time to search for a prospect's pains. Large accounts demand account planning and finding coaches to direct you through the maze of different levels. Instead these salespeople were selling features rather than building relationships.

Mistakes continued to be made and some very good managers lessened the blows from the fallout. Whenever I was feeling down and in need of some support, one manager took me for long lunches in some of the best restaurants. He listened and planted seeds. He protected his sales force against the internal politics and always gave us the benefit of the doubt. Another time I was in trouble with senior management for having made some unwanted comments and a senior manager told me not to worry – that he would take care of it. These managers supported their sales force and attracted good salespeople to the company. Good managers are good for the company and are good for the staff.

"When one door closes another door opens; but we so often look so long and so regretfully upon the closed door, that we do not see the ones which open for us." = **Alexander Graham Bell**

Managing salespeople: **Managing salespeople with bad working habits can be frustrating.**

Chapter Eleven
The Top Ten Lists

Having read the chapters on the sales process, networking, cold calling and what it takes to be a professional salesperson, all you need to do is to concentrate on the following 30+ points to be the best salesperson you can possibly be. Allow yourself 10 weeks to apply these concepts and then measure the progress you have made.

Top 10 most important things to do to be a successful professional salesperson

1. Learn the art of networking and cold calling at high levels.
2. Qualify again and again each hot prospect at every step of the sale.
3. Do not let up – after a sale has been won, go out and prospect on the strength of all that confidence. Keep your sales funnel full of prospects at different stages of closing.
4. Build good relationships with customers and think like a consultant. Work toward creating a symbiotic relationship or partnership.

5. Keep notes of your daily activities in order to manage your time well and review them on a regular basis. Take a course in time management to help improve productivity.

6. Spend the least possible amount of time in the office between 9 a.m. and 5 p.m. Keep your non-selling activities (planning, strategizing) for outside of office hours.

7. Learn about and observe body language, and work on empathy.

8. Search out the right coaches in large accounts and take care of them.

9. Find the customer's "pains." Focus less on your product's features/benefits and more on solving a customer's problems and adapting your product or service to his needs.

10. Know your competition. Do your own competitive analysis of their strengths and weaknesses.

Three additional items of importance on the non-selling side of sales are:

1. Review the annual sales objectives in your contract. Take time to understand them and to figure out which are the most profitable. Review each point with your manager.

2. Respect your sales team, give them recognition and communicate your ideas.

3. Like baseball players in spring training, sharpen your skills and add new ones by taking courses, listening to tapes and reading books on selling.

Top 10 most important things
to do to win a sale

1. First establish if the prospect or customer has a project and a budget for it.
2. Work with your manager to qualify the account.
3. Build an account plan appropriate to the size of the prospective sale.
4. Research the company and their competition via Web sites and search engines. Learn about their values, their problems and their objectives. Do a SWOT.
5. Familiarize yourself with the structure of the organization and learn how to reach the top people.
6. Identify the incumbent supplier and find out what your closest competitors are doing.
7. Never forget the importance of the administrative assistant/secretary in your pursuit of the sale.
8. Look for at least one coach, and preferably more coaches, within the target company who can be your guide and inform you about any changes, i.e., shift of power, promotions, change of personnel, etc.
9. Confirm who the real decision-makers are.
10. Consider sending an unsolicited proposal rather than waiting for a request for proposal (RFP).

Top 10 things to do to lose a sale

1. Exaggerate a situation or tell an out-and-out lie. It will come back to haunt you.
2. Arrive a few minutes late for your meetings. Do not look eager or hungry by being prompt.
3. Do not confirm your appointment the day before. Assume your prospect/customer is as keen to meet you, as you are to meet him or her.
4. Do not listen to what the prospect/customer is saying, or try to discover his pains. You already have your own preconceived ideas.
5. Make promises, even if you are not certain of being able to keep them, just so the customer remains happy for the time being. They shoot messengers (and salespeople), don't they?
6. Show your independence. You have spent enough time on the prospect/customer and there are other companies that are really hot for your product. If he wants it, he has your number.
7. Wait for the customer to call you if he needs anything or to inform you of a new project in the works. After all, he is already a customer and would not consider talking to your competition.

8. If you call your customer, you may learn of some problems or dissatisfaction with your product. Avoid situations like this and let the customer work out his own problems.

9. Be a cherry picker. Wait for the right prospect to drop into your lap and meanwhile, set up executive lunches or nights out on the town with important-looking people who can make you look good.

10. Ignore the "little" people in a company. Deal only with those at the top. They are the only ones that matter.

Afterword

Bringing it all together

Depending on your experience, parts of this text will appear self-evident. Each reader will naturally bring his or her unique blend of experience to the task. The real key to getting the most out of this book is to knit the larger fabric of this book into your particular strengths. Advance from one chapter to the next, methodically putting into practice the strategies or points that address areas where you have the most to gain, concentrating on one or two at a time. Applying the new, along with your proven techniques, may not make you a "powerhouse" in sales, but you will be amazed at the progress.

Keep the book handy as a reference tool. The Top 10 lists can be entered into a personal digital assistant (PDA) or posted on an office wall as a checklist for every prospect and client account.

Good luck in winning many new customers. But as everyone in professional sales knows, it is not luck but hard work that wins a sale.

"I am a great believer in luck, and I find the harder I work, the more I have of it." – **Stephen Leacock**

List of illustrations

1. Choosing your prospects: *Most people can list a dozen or more suspects. We usually gravitate to the one with whom we feel most comfortable or to the most accessible prospect but not necessarily the best. Qualify all and choose to approach those with the most potential first.*

2. Using your contacts: *When we are looking for a job or assistance of any kind, we first ask friends and family. Often we overlook acquaintances and their contacts in our search.*

3. Networking: *Make contact with potential buyers in the industry by attending cocktails and business luncheons, working with your alumni association or a charity. Networking makes winning new customers so much easier.*

4. Cold calling, Cold: *A "cold" cold call is rarely used in professional sales. Usually professional salespeople will know something about the prospect or will have searched the Internet. Nevertheless in exceptional times when there is no other choice, the effort may yet result in a sale.*

5. Cold calling, Hot: *A "hot" cold call is useful in selling at a professional level. Time and money spent on preparing before telephoning or meeting with a prospect is relative to the size of the potential sale.*

6. Cold calling, Hot-Hot: *A "hot-hot" cold call requires extensive and thorough preparation. The resulting confidence and knowledge of the company and its pains will guarantee a better reception from the prospect during the telephone call or meeting.*

7. Cold calling at high levels: *An experienced salesperson knows the competition is very likely connected to top management. The chance of success for those who are is very good. To alleviate any apprehension in approaching the higher levels, research the company and its industry and come well prepared to provide solutions to their pains.*

8. Gatekeeper: *An obstacle to reaching the decision-maker is the gatekeeper. The path of the inexperienced salesperson is blocked by the secretary/administrative assistant. One way around the problem is waiting until the gatekeeper has left work; another way is to try to work with him or her.*

9. Finding a coach: *A coach inside or outside the organization is an ally who helps you find your way through the company maze. He understands company politics and may know who the real decision-maker is.*

10. Finding the decision-maker: *Without the help of a coach, the identity of the decision-maker is not always obvious. If you have no contacts within the company, attempt to make contact with the CFO first. The CFO sometimes goes under the name of Vice-President of Finance or Controller – the person who controls the money – and can point you in the right direction.*

11. Finding the pains: *Come prepared with open-ended questions. Know the prospect's competition and some of the large customers. Conduct a brainstorming session with an industry expert.*

12. What is the competition doing? *Most large companies do competitive analysis. To do your own, check the Web often for information on who competes in what field. Ask a customer or prospect about your competition, find out who is wooing them and talk to the competition at any event where you may meet them.*

13. Negotiations: *If you are not an experienced negotiator, take a course, read books on negotiating and/ or seek advice from a senior person in your organization. Otherwise you may pay a hefty price when closing deals.*

14. Closing the deal: *Some salespeople focus on getting the contract not really knowing if it is possible to do the job on time or if it is profitable. This is usually considered the most complex part of the sales process. If each step in the sales process has been followed the customer and you, as a consultant, have made the decision together.*

15. Customer references: *A satisfied customer, who has been well treated, returns the favour by telling others about your great product and/or service.*

16. Taking care of the customer: *Spending time with a customer inside and outside the workplace is essential to building a good relationship. From these occasions come repeat orders and good references. So spoil the customer.*

17. Listening to the customer's needs: *Often we do not listen carefully enough or know how to listen, or worse, ignore customers when they talk about their pains.*

18. Partners working together: *To offer a complete solution to a prospect or customer's requirements, to access new markets or simply to increase earnings, a* *partnership can be a valuable sales strategy. Finding partners is much like building friendships, and both can be mutually beneficial.*

19. Honesty: *Honesty has always been the best policy. Good principles are the foundation for continued sales success, and exaggeration is to be avoided. Tell it like it is.*

20. Why become a salesperson? *A job in sales offers advancement, flexible hours, creativity, good earnings, challenges and more. It calls for endurance, perseverance and confidence. It is never static.*

21. Time management: *Time is a fleeting commodity. It is far easier to allow events to decide your next actions but more practical and rewarding to plan them.*

22. Empathy: *Not everyone is capable of putting themselves in someone else's shoes. It can be painful as well as difficult.*

23. Body language: *A prospect's body language may be more revealing than her words. She scratched the top of her head and looked away but she did not cite any problems. There may be different interpretations of these actions.*

24. Managing salespeople: *Managing salespeople with bad working habits can be frustrating.*

Glossary

Account Plan – A document profiling an organization and its industry. It includes an organizational chart, company objectives, a planned strategy and tactics set out to win the account.

Blue Bird – A sale that is made as a result of a customer or prospect contacting a company to purchase its product. Very little effort is required to win the account.

Body Language – A subtle physical action or stance that is perceived and its meaning understood without any words being spoken.

Business Development – Another term for sales.

Call Sheet – A one-page document used to help prompt the caller in his dialogue during a cold call to a suspect. Following the greeting are the hot buttons – choice words to keep the suspect interested.

Coach (inside) – A person who provides information on the prospect – its problems, people and politics – to help a salesperson make a sale.

Cold Call – An initial call made to a prospect after little or no preparation.

Cold Call, "Hot" – An initial call made to a prospect after having done some research on the company, its people and its competition.

Cold Call, "Hot-Hot" – An initial call made to a prospect after 40 to 80 hours of thorough research and preparation in order to ensure the prospect will have a strong interest in your product.

Customer Pains – A prospect's problems and obstacles, objectives and strategies.

Empathy – In sales, one takes on the problems of a prospect or customer, understands their pains beyond what is normally expected of a supplier and looks for a solution.

ERP software – Enterprise Resource Planning (ERP) software. One description is that of controlling all the data in a company by standardizing one system for the front end and using one data source for the back end.

Executive Summary – Located at the beginning of a proposal, it contains the most relevant information – a customer's problems and a solution to these problems, the customer's investment and time guideline.

Gatekeeper – Usually an administrative assistant who has the responsibility for screening unimportant callers so as to free up a manager's time.

Hot Buttons – Subject matter important to prospects that will hold their attention; e.g., lowering costs and increasing profits.

Networking – Meeting new people for the purpose of increasing the prospect base or helping to advance the sales process.

Non-Stop computer – A computer built with duplicate hardware components. If one unit fails, the operation continues on the second CPU, disc, power supply, etc. Best known for the non-stop computer was Tandem Computers (now part of Hewlett Packard).

OEM (Other Equipment Manufacturer) – A company that takes another company's product, possibly makes some changes and resells it.

Passing the Puck – In hockey the player who passes the puck to the one who scores gets an assist. In sales, as in hockey, the one who benefits (scorer) remembers the assist and may reciprocate.

Payback – The length of time it takes to recover the initial cost of a project, without regard to the time value of money.

PDA (Personal Digital Assistant) – A handheld computer small enough to fit into a pocket. It replaces an address and personal phone book, weekly agenda, calculator and notepad.

Prospect – A person or company that has the potential of becoming a customer.

Reseller – Similar to an OEM, but a reseller sells someone's product without any modification to the product.

RFP/RFQ (request for price/quote) – A document sent to suppliers requesting proposals to answer the specific needs laid out.

ROI (return on investment) – An investment of $1,000 that generates $200 on an annual basis has an ROI of 20 per cent (200/1000).

Sales Process – A series of recommended steps that begins with a search for prospective customer and ends with a satisfied customer. Every step includes verification of the process, by way of qualifying the prospect.

Search Engine – Computer software on the Internet that provides fairly complete information on every subject imaginable.

Suspect – Often confused with a prospect, a suspect is a possible customer as is any name in the telephone book. A suspect becomes a prospect at the beginning of the sales process by way of a positive contact or a meeting.

SWOT (Strength, Weakness, Opportunities, Threats) – An analysis of a prospect or customer to help uncover their needs so as to propose a viable solution.

Symbiotic relationship – A mutually supportive relationship in which two partners (customer and supplier) benefit equally.

War Room – A so-called room where a number of people meet for the purpose of discussing strategies and tactics regarding how best to win an account or retain a customer.

Bibliography

Auer, J. T. *The Joy of Selling.* Toronto: Stoddard, (1989).

Ciaramicoli, Arthur P., Ketcham, Katherine. *The Power of Empathy*. New York: Dutton Books, Penguin, (2000).

Hopkins, Tom with Wilson, Hersch. *Changing the Game: The New Way to Sell.* New York: Fireside Books, Simon & Schuster, (1987).

Holden, Jim. *Power Base Selling*. New York: John Wiley & Sons, (1990).

Hopkins, Tom. *How to Master the Art of Selling*. New York: Werner Books, (1982).

Mercer, David. *High-level Selling*. Houston: Gulf Publishing Co, (1990).

Sandler, David H. *You Can't Teach a Kid to Ride a Bike at a Seminar*. New York: Dutton Books, Penguin, (1995).

For further information, to arrange an interview with the author, for special events, lectures and seminars, etc., write to:

MLCIA Publications
50 St-Charles
P.O. Box 26711
Beaconsfield, Quebec
Canada H9W 6G7
or
e-mail at: info@mlcipub.com

To order copies of "Winning New Customers," *visit our website* www.mlcipub.com *or write to the above address with the following information:*

Please send us _____ copies of "Winning New Customers." *Enclosed is a cheque made payable to MLCIA Publication Inc. in the amount of* $_____ CDN or $_____ US or $_____ EU

Full Name _____

Address _____

City _____ **Prov. /State** _____

Postal/Zip Code _____ **Country** _____

Tel: _____ **E-mail** _____

$27.95 CDN   21.95US   18.95 EU

For the province of Quebec please add PST and GST. For all other provinces, please add GST. Outside Canada, remittance of taxes is your responsibility.

For special pricing of orders above 10 books, please e-mail.

Allow two to five weeks for delivery.

"Marc Chabot is the master salesman. Through his advice we were able to grow our company by 200 per cent in two and half years by signing deals with the major players in our field. In this book Marc reveals a lot of the practical action-oriented wisdom that he accumulated in his 25 years working and closing major deals. Read it, apply it and see your customer base grow in size. This is the book to read if you want to reach the major accounts and keep them."

- Shibl Mourad, President, Sequence Technologies

"Marc has been my mentor for more than 15 years. From hiring me to helping me move into sales management, he has provided me with tremendous insight as to how to be successful in any business endeavour. When a new account is in his sight, there is no stopping him. Meeting a potential client, Marc masters the essentials of listening and checking his ego at the door."

- Richard Martel, President, Decimal Technologies Inc.

"Marc has worked with me over the last few years as a consultant. I have watched how he networks and helps close large deals through his proven cold calling and networking techniques. He has also trained some of our people with excellent success. Marc knows how to build networks in industries unfamiliar to him at the outset. He is a great salesman and the best door opener in the industry."

- Alan Katiya, CA, KPMG